Tynan

Welcome to
Canada

by Alison Auch

Content and Reading Adviser: Mary Beth Fletcher, Ed.D.
Educational Consultant/Reading Specialist
The Carroll School, Lincoln, Massachusetts

Spyglass BOOKS

COMPASS POINT BOOKS

Minneapolis, Minnesota

Compass Point Books
3722 West 50th Street, #115
Minneapolis, MN 55410

Visit Compass Point Books on the Internet at *www.compasspointbooks.com*
or e-mail your request to *custserv@compasspointbooks.com*

Project Manager: Rebecca Weber McEwen
Editor: Heidi Schoof   ·
Photo Selectors: Rebecca Weber McEwen and Heidi Schoof
Designers: Jaime Martens and Les Tranby
Illustrator: Svetlana Zhurkina

Library of Congress Cataloging-in-Publication Data

Auch, Alison.
 Welcome to Canada / by Alison Auch.
     p. cm. — (Spyglass books)
Contents: Where is Canada? — A hunting way of life — Bundle up! — Old
and new food — Playing games — "How the crow got daylight" — Fun facts.
  ISBN 0-7565-0372-8 (hardcover)
 1. Canada—Social life and customs—Juvenile literature.
 [1. Canada-—Social life and customs.] I. Title. II. Series.
  F1021.2 .A84 2002
  971—dc21
                        2002002750

Contents

Where Is Canada?

Welcome to my country!
I live in Canada.
I want to tell you
about my beautiful home.

Canadian Flag

Did You Know?

Canada is the second
largest country in the world.
Russia is the biggest.

ARCTIC OCEAN

CANADA

PACIFIC
OCEAN

ATLANTIC
OCEAN

N
W   E
S

0   500 miles

0   500 km

At Home

Canada has big cities
and lots of open land.
My family lives in
a small town. We live
far from the closest city.

Most Canadians live in big cities.

Some people live in small towns.

At Work

Outside the big cities, most people work in the outdoors. My dad has a fishing boat.

My mom has a restaurant like this one. She loves to cook!

In Canada, many people work in fishing, farming, *mining*, or *lumbering*.

Let's Eat!

My family eats a lot of fish. We also eat beef, chicken, and pork. Our vegetables come from farms in central Canada.

Out in the country, some people hunt
animals such as *caribou* for food.

Bundle Up!

Canada has long cold winters. We like to wear jeans and sweaters. To keep warm, we wear heavy coats, hats, and boots.

It is dangerous to go out in
the cold without the right clothes.

Dark and Light

In Canada, it is dark in the winter. Some places only get an hour or two of daylight each day!

In northern Canada, it is light outside almost all the time in the summer.

Many people like to go
cross-country skiing.

Fun Facts

Some Canadian cities have snow festivals.

The bright colors that flash across the night sky in Canada are called northern lights.

The native people
of northern Canada
are the Inuit. They
are not called
Eskimos anymore.

Some Canadians
compete in
sled dog races.

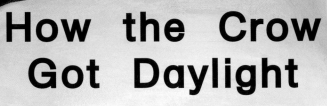

How the Crow Got Daylight

(an Inuit legend)

Long ago, the people
had no daylight.
They were tired of living
in the dark all the time.

The people begged Crow
to bring them daylight.

Crow agreed to help.
He flew south to find light.
He saw a baby playing
with a shiny ball of daylight.
Crow stole it.

On his way home, Crow dropped bits of daylight for each village. There was enough daylight for half the year. The people were very happy.

21

Glossary

caribou–a four-legged animal
with antlers. It is also called
a "reindeer."

cross-country skiing–to ski across
land instead of down a hill
or mountain

lumbering–cutting down trees and
getting them ready to use to
make other things

mining–digging under the ground
for things such as coal or silver

sled dog–a dog specially trained
to pull sleds

Learn More

Books

Ekoomiak, Normee. *Arctic Memories.*
New York: Henry Holt, 1988.

Fowler, Allan. *The Top and Bottom of the World.* New York: Children's Press, 1997.

Hancock, Lyn. *Nunavut.* Minneapolis, Minn.: Lerner Publications, 1995.

Web Site

www.ainc-inac.gc.ca/ks/english/
index_e.html

Index

GR: G
Word Count: 195

From Alison Auch

Reading and writing are my favorite things to do. When I'm not reading or writing, I like to go to the mountains or play with my little girl, Chloe.